HOW DO I LOOK?
SENNAH YEE

How Do I Look?
By Sennah Yee
ISBN 978-1-988355-08-5

Copyright © Sennah Yee, 2017
Second Edition, Third Printing

Published by Metatron Press
Montréal, Québec
www.metatron.press

All rights reserved

Editor | Jay Ritchie
Cover art | Christine Shan Shan Hou

We acknowledge the support of the Canada Council for the Arts,
which last year invested $153 million to bring the arts to Canadians
throughout the country.

HOW DO I LOOK?
SENNAH YEE

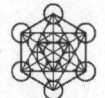

HOW DO I LOOK?

MEDUSA 11

MOTHERLODE 12

SKINNY-DIPPING 13

FROM ANONYMOUS ANSWERS TO 14

PROM 15

NEVER HAVE I EVER 16

WHEN I WAS YOUR AGE 17

BE PREPARED 18

MULAN (1998) 19

CHO CHANG 20

BACK TO THE FUTURE (1985) 21

NEXT LIFE 22

BOND "GIRLS" PT. 1: LUCIA 23

BOND "GIRLS" PT. 2: ESTRELLA 24

EX MACHINA (2015) 25

THE FAST AND THE FURIOUS (2001) 26

THERE WILL BE BLOOD (2007) 27

BREAKFAST AT TIFFANY'S (1961) 28

WINGED TIPS 29

SIXTEEN CANDLES (1984) 30

LOST IN TRANSLATION (2003) 31

GILMORE GIRLS REVIVAL 32

PREVIOUSLY ON *MAD MEN* 33

INTIMATES 34

GET HOME SAFE 35

WHITE WIFE 36

MAKE ME A STAR 37

WORKING FROM HOME 38

PLAYING *GTA V* AT 4 A.M. 39

A WORKING LIST OF SEXUAL AWAKENINGS 40

MY TYPE 41

FLOWER CROWN SNAPCHAT FILTER 42

#FESTIVALSZN 43

INTERNET SAFETY 44

DIAL-UP INTERNET SOUNDS 45

DOLLZ MANIA 46

AND AFTER ALL YOU'RE MY WONDERWALL 47

MYSPACE.COM 48

THIS JOURNAL HAS BEEN DELETED AND PURGED 49

THERAPY 50

BRUGES 51

ANTWERP 52

BRUSSELS 53

BERLIN 54

PARIS 55

WORDS I KNOW IN CHINESE 56

WORDS I DO NOT KNOW IN CHINESE 57

NEW YORK CITY 58

BAR HARBOUR 59

MEDOMAK 60

TEXAS FOREVER 61

WHITE SEATMATES ON CHINA EASTERN FLIGHT 207 62

SIEM REAP 63

THE BEACH 64

THE DESERT 65

THE TOP OF THE MOUNTAIN 66

WHAT KIND OF ANIMAL ARE YOU? BUZZFEED QUIZ 67

FLORA 68

FAUNA 69

THINGS THAT HAVE MORE HEARTS THAN ME 70

BLADE RUNNER (1982) 71

HER (2013) 72

REAR WINDOW (1954) 73

VIVRE SA VIE (1962) 74

IN THE MOOD FOR LOVE (2000) 75

LOVE 76

REAL LOVE 77

TRUE LOVE 78

CRITERIA FOR CRAZY 79

HOW DO I LOOK?

MEDUSA

Beauty, power, and confidence without gaze. Then, a man holds up a mirror and kills her. There is nothing mythical about that.

MOTHERLODE

Sarah and I always played *The Sims* with versions of us, our sk8er boi crushes, our celeb crushes (*Fight Club*-era Brad Pitt and Edward Norton), and our enemies. My older sister helped us download cool mods: makeup from My Chemical Romance music videos, tattoos and dermal piercings, BDSM outfits before we knew what the letters stood for, and Cloud from *Final Fantasy VII*'s hair. We made our sk8er boi crushes fall in love with us in minutes. We took turns woohoo-ing in the hot tub with Brad and Edward and giggled at the pixels. We made our enemies pee themselves and die by fire. We accidentally fell in love with each other and had to Google how to undo it. We cheated so we were forever full, rich, and young. We forgot that the sk8er bois never talked to us, that Brad and Edward didn't look like that anymore, that we kind of felt sorry for our enemies.

SKINNY-DIPPING

I had never seen my friends naked. He said he had never seen nipples as dark as mine. Knowing his dating and porn history, I believed him.

**FROM ANONYMOUS ANSWERS TO:
WHAT IS YOUR FAVOURITE MEMORY OF LAST
SUMMER? WHAT DID YOU LIKE/HATE ABOUT
YOUR FIRST CRUSH? WRITE SOMETHING TO
SOMEONE YOU MISS.**

After pool-hopping fully clothed, we got stuck in the rain. It was August. I got to see where she grew up: Chinatown bars, the spa across the street, a haunted house. I liked her dark hair, her ambivalence towards me. I've rarely laughed harder. Lots to hate, too: teeth stained yellow. Constant wandering and coming back. The first time we slept in the same bed, I wanted her to have wanted me more. She called me "the one that got away" even though she always left me behind. I walked into the lake the morning after. It was hot and my feet were dust. My skin was sore. Hate takes a long time to soak up.

PROM

I bought us pearl earrings for $5 from an elderly vendor in Chinatown. I told him how neither of us had ever owned anything pearl before. He knew they were fake, and so did I, and so did you, but it didn't matter. Later, you spilled Smirnoff all over the gown you borrowed from your sister. I tried not to stare at the lace and sequins of your bra seeping through the soaked fabric. Having eyes only for you is just a glamorous way of saying that I cannot see.

NEVER HAVE I EVER

Everyone knew I'd slept with my high school girlfriend but everyone still called me a virgin. "You drink if you have, not if you haven't." "Either you are, or you aren't." "Either you did, or you didn't." I drink extra.

WHEN I WAS YOUR AGE

I couldn't spell my favourite colour (fuchsia). I thought beach glass was real. I thought rubber plants were real. I wanted Santa Claus to knock on my front door and ask permission before coming into my house. I thought my dad couldn't cry. I took a paint sample from Home Depot called "Moon Tide" because it was a free bookmark. I thought there were multiple moons that came out on different nights. I thought Sting was hot. I thought "Toronto" on a globe meant my exact house. I thought I would buy my exact house from my parents and live in it forever. I thought we could live forever so long as I blew out all the candles on my birthday cake.

BE PREPARED

In Girl Guides we do a craft where we make felt and yarn replicas of ourselves. I cut a piece of beige felt into the shape of my heart-shaped face. I draw my round nose and eyes. I comb through the yarn pile for my hair, but there are only yellow, brown, and orange. Volunteer Mom "didn't think to bring any black yarn." I'm stuck with brown. A hovering Girl Guide informs me, "Your hair isn't brown. And your eyes aren't that big in real life." Next morning, I see my mom at the kitchen table, snipping off my brown yarn hair into a pile. Next to the pile is a glue stick, along with another pile of yarn—jet-black, thick, lovely.

MULAN (1998)

For my sixth birthday I got a *Mulan* backpack, *Mulan* lunchbox, *Mulan* PJs, *Mulan* Halloween costume, and three *Mulan* dolls, each in different outfits, and with varying lengths of black hair. Sometimes when I played with the dolls in my bed, I would notice a stray hair on my pillow, and I liked that I didn't know whose it was. One day when hanging up my *Mulan* backpack in the cubby, a classmate said, "You just like her because you look like her." I was embarrassed, but I didn't know why. I wore a plain backpack for the rest of the year.

CHO CHANG

I made my dad help me record an audition tape even though I wasn't British, or even an actress. But I'm Asian, and for once, that's what fit. I sat with my mom and marked all of Cho Chang's lines in *Goblet of Fire* with electric blue Post-its. When I read them all aloud back-to-back, they only added up to 17 seconds of dialogue. Still, I recited them over and over like a mantra.

BACK TO THE FUTURE (1985)

Back to kindergarten when he pulled his eyes up to mock mine. Back to fourth grade when he asked me to translate a line from *Dragon Ball Z*. Back to sixth grade when they asked if Jackie Chan was my dad. Back to ninth grade when I let him write me stupid racist love poems comparing me to sweet and sour sauce. Back to frosh week when he complimented my good English. Back to yesterday at the movie theater when he yelled, "Hey chink hey chink I wanna fuck you in the ass," and I cried to you over the phone in the bathroom. Now, I pull his eyes back down. Now, I tell him to use Google Translate, and I'm not Japanese. Now, I tell them yeah, Jackie Chan's my dad, and Lucy Liu's my mom. Now, I write poems about his stupid racist love poems. Now, I tell him his English is great too, but his manners, not so much. Now, I still cry to you over the phone in the bathroom, but now, I know it's okay to do this.

NEXT LIFE

In my next life I will not need bleach. In my next life I will get the girl. In my next life they will buy me drinks. In my next life I will not shave. In my next life I will be Hollywood. In my next life TV will be a mirror. In my next life I will be justified. In my next life I will not be asked any questions. In my next life my self-love will not have to be self-made. In my next life I will kiss and bite every hand that feeds me. In my next life I will be comforted that those hands will not flinch or bleed.

BOND "GIRLS" PT. 1: LUCIA

Everyone loves older men and even older cities. But women must be girls, and preferably girls from out of town. But I've lived here my whole life. And when you died, I fell asleep and dreamt of somewhere with no men and no time. I ate creatures from the sea with no silver and no company. I taught myself to drive, in a car with no roof and no brand. My hair was greying, knotting in the wind, but I did not reach out to brush it. I was alone, but I was not left behind.

BOND "GIRLS" PT. 2: ESTRELLA

I used to like it when you'd call me mysterious. Mysterious is oxblood lipstick. Mysterious is ink peeking out from a cuff. Mysterious is smoking on a rooftop that is not yours. Mysterious is gauze curtains pooling onto the floor. Mysterious is a faint moon while the sun is still out. Mysterious is a languid crowd. Mysterious is wearing roses, lace, bone. But mysterious is foreign. Mysterious is mute. Mysterious is nude. Mysterious is being left behind in a room that is not yours. Mysterious is being imagined. Mysterious is an excuse to write me off.

***EX MACHINA* (2015)**

Would you touch me, love me, fuck me more if I was glass, chrome, silicone?

THE FAST AND THE FURIOUS (2001)

My mom is named after Rita Hayworth but has seen none of her films. I am named after a Formula 1 racecar driver who died in a crash during a race just two years after I was born, and just last year I let my driver's license expire without ever getting behind the wheel. I make up for all this by winning *Mario Kart*, watching movies with cars and babes, and having you drive me around in your boss's convertible that he lends you when he vacations in Lyon. Paused at a red light with you, a guy crossing the street tells me to smile. You roll the roof back up and I feel everyone's lingering gaze. There is that satisfying mix of envy and respect and disgust, and I finally understood the appeal of stupid things like unscathed leather and purring engines and road head. Next week I retake the driver's test and when I get my photo I.D. taken, the guy at the booth tells me to stop smiling. I have to.

THERE WILL BE BLOOD (2007)

Sometimes when customers are rude to me, I fantasize that I'm Daniel Plainview and think about what kinds of delicious Oscar-worthy threats I could slobber at them, such as: I will write about you. And: I won't write about you.

BREAKFAST AT TIFFANY'S (1961)

He mentioned once that his ex looks like Audrey. When she sings "Moon River," I remember my third-grade piano recital where I hit the wrong last chords. My fingers ached trying to reach all the keys. My dad filmed it, even though I had told him not to. When Mickey Rooney squawks in buck-toothed yellowface, I catch my reflection in the black pockets of the TV screen. My eyes are even narrower when I'm embarrassed. *"How do I look?"* Holly Golightly asks. She's a movie star.

WINGED TIPS

I only let you put makeup on me because I had a crush on you. "How do I look?" I asked. You didn't let me look at the mirror. You closed the window with the YouTube tutorial. You rubbed everything away. The thing about monolids is that you can work on them for ages, only to look up at your reflection and see zero progress. But it's there. You couldn't see it then, and neither could I. But I can see it now.

***SIXTEEN CANDLES* (1984)**

When I was 13 and obsessed with the '80s, I watched all of Molly Ringwald's movies with my mom—except she didn't let me watch this one. She said it wasn't because I was too young, but because of Long Duk Dong. I said, "It's okay, I can handle it." She said, "I know, but I don't want you to have to."

***LOST IN TRANSLATION* (2003)**

How come my alienation isn't soft and beautiful?

GILMORE GIRLS REVIVAL

Or, revival of white people telling my mom, my older sister, my younger sister, my cousin, my aunt, my friend, my piano teacher, and me that we remind them *sooo* much of Lane.

PREVIOUSLY ON *MAD MEN*

I watch Betty Draper smoke and shoot pigeons in her white nightgown while I eat crunchy Cheetos and shoot the shit in Roots Kids sweatpants.

INTIMATES

After finishing *Boardwalk Empire*, I bought my first and only slip. The woman at the lingerie store said, "He'll love it," but I love it even more. It's burgundy, the same hue as my mom's knit hat, my prom dress, my favourite and only tube of lipstick, but with gold trim. It makes my breasts bumpy with lace, my belly cool and smooth.

GET HOME SAFE

It's what women say to each other instead of "See you later." When I get home safe and take off my clothes, I can smell a mix of all my friends' perfumes on my neck from hugging them close all night. I inhale. I exhale.

WHITE WIFE

"That's when you know you've made it." I don't know this friend of a friend, and don't want to, so I bite my tongue, sip from my melted ice cubes. I write an angry text to my white boyfriend about it. I sprinkle it with emojis to lighten my tone. I think about how white girls envy how easily I tan. I think about how when I was younger, I'd hide under the shadows of trees, beach umbrellas, pedestals. I think about bleach. I nix the emojis before sending.

MAKE ME A STAR

Gazing up at me, you know I'm already long gone.

WORKING FROM HOME

Cheesecake for breakfast and yesterday's McDonald's dollar drink. I'm linking three separate friends to a video of a fox making and eating a six-layer sandwich. You're trying to find the meme that had us laughing so hard last night that we woke up the cat. Which reminds me, I need to make an Instagram for my cat. I'll do it after we're done pirating *Pirates of the Caribbean 4* because apparently there's a *Pirates of the Caribbean 4*. I'm trying to be too edgy while crafting a cover letter for a *VICE* magazine social media job and state that my dream job is to do social media for Denny's. I don't get either job.

PLAYING *GTA V* AT 4 A.M.

I don't think I'm good at this. I'm blowing all my money on clothes and tattoos and I keep stopping to gaze at the sunset—in the game, I mean—and I'm running around with nowhere to go and everyone on my back. I search sunrise/sunset times on an online forum and find this: *It takes awhile for the sun to make it past the mountains. Go to the east shoreline at 4 a.m. and you'll notice that's when it starts to get brighter.* I'm panicking about missing the sunset over the beach, but then I realize it's okay, because the beach will always be there, and actually, the sun is always there; even if I can't always see it. The thought makes me misty-eyed—in real life, I mean.

A WORKING LIST OF SEXUAL AWAKENINGS

- Jessica Simpson and Nick Lachey on the cover of *Us Weekly*
- Men kissing in Christina Aguilera's "Beautiful" music video
- Kylie Minogue's white hooded jumpsuit in the "Can't Get You Outta My Head" music video
- Nightrider Kim in Lil' Kim's "How Many Licks?" music video
- Britney Spears's sheer sparkly bodysuit in the "Toxic" music video
- J. Lo's green Versace dress
- Some guy's feet in Fiona Apple's "Criminal" music video
- Brittany Murphy rubbing Egyptian cotton sheets on her boyfriend in *Uptown Girls*
- Milla Jovovich in *Zoolander*
- Serena Williams
- Wentworth Miller's tattoos in *Prison Break*
- Wentworth Miller in Mariah Carey's music videos
- Mariah Carey in Mariah Carey's music videos
- Captain Jack Sparrow
- T.I. – Whatever You Like.mp3
- Toronto Roller Derby

MY TYPE

Women who would make Drake cry.

FLOWER CROWN SNAPCHAT FILTER

My skin is lighter and my eyes are wider and my nose is narrower and I secretly relish this for a maximum of 10 seconds.

#FESTIVALSZN

Hiding under some shade, waiting for The Killers to come on, I overhear: "*Marco Polo*'s on Netflix. It's like *Game of Thrones*, but like, Asian. And some of the Asian guys are actually kinda hot?!?!" I sit up and see white girls wearing bindis sitting with white guys wearing pointy straw Chinese hats. I take off my sunglasses, my hat, shoot them death stares with my little eyes, black hair down. They don't see me.

INTERNET SAFETY

My dad taught me to never give out my real name, age, address, or photos. This seemed obvious to me. My fake birthday entry was always my crush's birthday plus a random year from the early 1900s. I spent hours making my avatars look like everything, anything but myself. It didn't matter how people (mis)pronounced my name, how young I was, how squinty my eyes were. I can't remember my crush's birthday anymore. He was a Gemini, but that doesn't help enough. According to my fake birthday, I'm dead, anyway.

DIAL-UP INTERNET SOUNDS

Like diamond rainstorms on Jupiter, the seaside snarling in the dark, you hanging up on me right as I'm saying goodbye.

DOLLZ MANIA

My intro to nudity was those early-'00s doll-maker sites. I was mesmerized by the dollz' base bodies with their legginess, pinched waists, belly button slits, and most of all their weird little pink pixel nipples. I would click + drag + drop + click + drag + drop + click + drag + drop my favourite slutty outfits and align them perfectly onto their base bodies. Micro miniskirts, sheer tops, spaghetti straps that were forbidden in grade school. My base body is dry and short and hairy. My base body is moisturized and plucked and shaved and stretched and covered up and stripped. My base body is dragged + dropped around online and offline. My base body is getting hungry, tired, and old.

AND AFTER ALL YOU'RE MY WONDERWALL

During my MSN days, I felt prettier looking at a webcam than looking at a mirror. Looking at myself look at myself being looked at.

MYSPACE.COM

High angles would do nothing for the gap between my breasts. I would use the flash to wash my features out. I would open my eyes far and wide. Think doe-eyed. Think Audrey. Think Zooey. Think mine are going to fall out of their sockets. When Bambi's mom got shot, my sister made my mom stop the VCR and put on *Mulan* instead. *"Don't look back. Keep running. Keep running."*

THIS JOURNAL HAS BEEN DELETED AND PURGED

I have nightmares of LiveJournal friends from my teens finding me now. I would disappoint them.

THERAPY

Therapy is wearing all black. Therapy is sheer glass. Therapy is eye contact. Therapy is scales of one to ten. Therapy is forced chemistry. Therapy is making you squirm. Therapy is running on the spot. Therapy is counted on a shiny wristwatch. Therapy is telling you to go. Therapy is letting you stay. Therapy is lush furniture. Therapy is sleet on windows. Therapy is sleepy mountains. Therapy is far away from you.

BRUGES

It's a fairytale pop-up book here except with no bad guys. There's a cute fellow Canadian in my tour group who tells me that's the window that Colin Farrell jumped out of in that movie. We take a picture together in front of that window even though I don't really like Colin Farrell and haven't seen that movie. We get free chocolate samples and eat them near a canal. Cute fellow Canadian tells me that I don't *look* Canadian; where am I *really* from? The free chocolate gets stuck in my teeth. I stick my fingers into my mouth and pick it out in front of them. They grimace at me. I smile back, teeth bared.

ANTWERP

I walk alone for two hours to a recommended restaurant. There's a handwritten sign that says they're closed Tuesdays, Thursdays, and Sundays. It's Tuesday. There's a heat wave that day and a downpour that night. We share an umbrella home from the bar, but only I catch a cold.

BRUSSELS

I suggest a cheap Chinese restaurant to some fellow 20-somethings. They perk up at "cheap," but once we're there, they regret it. "Everyone here is Asian..." says one of the guys, nose wrinkling. "That's how you know it's good," I say. Later, he's too busy devouring his €3 fried rice to bite his tongue.

BERLIN

I need to discover sex, says some street art on the way to the disco-art-opening-DJ-funk-night. "*Konichiwa*," says some fucker on the U-Bahn. Chocolate milkshake cools my throat. "Kracauer was so right; clubs *are* like churches," we say jokingly, but we mean it. Apricot brandy gives me Asian glow. "I need to know what 'fuck' is in German, like, the verb," she says jokingly, but she means it. Watching *Possession* in an outdoor cinema fucks with my head. The wind makes ripples on the projector screen. "*Almost, almost,*" says Isabelle Adjani. *This is a dream*, says some street art on the way home.

PARIS

A group of guys yell *"nǐ hǎo"* at me on the Champs-Élysées with the same venom they would save for "cunt." My friend doesn't know how to comfort me but that's okay because neither do I. We find a side entrance to the Louvre with no lineup. Once inside, all the paintings blur together: bougie garden parties, pale angels, goddesses with rosy cheeks and nipples. *"Nǐ hǎo, nǐ hǎo, nǐ hǎo,"* rings through my head.

WORDS I KNOW IN CHINESE

Mother, father, older sister, younger sister, grandpa (mother's side), grandpa (father's side), grandma (mother's side), grandma (father's side), thank you, hello, one, two, three, four, five, six, happy new year, pork dumpling, shrimp dumpling, pork bun, turnip cake, porridge, expensive, fart, flower, overly kind, knock on wood, I'm going to chop your head in two halves.

WORDS I DO NOT KNOW IN CHINESE

No, I don't know, fuck off, shut up, help, how are you, I'm good, I'm sorry, I love you, I miss you, I don't speak Chinese, but I wish I spoke Chinese, because I love being Chinese.

NEW YORK CITY

I get clawed by a bodega cat and step in a tiny dog's huge pile of shit. I get all the big bridges mixed up. I get fish tempura tacos served by a waiter whose hand-poked leg tattoos remind me of you, but not as much as the way her kneecap pleats do. She gets beer on my lap and I get real Canadian and say, "Oh god, I'm so sorry."

BAR HARBOUR

I buy my own little lobster to eat by the water. It's cold and red and cheap and just for me. The breeze is bitter on my cheeks and makes my arm hair rise. But my black hair is warmed by the sun. I think I can see a storm, but it's far away. I will miss it.

MEDOMAK

You wake me up in the middle of the night to look at the phosphorescents in the ocean. I slip on a rock and slice my ankle. You tell me to let the waves lap at the wound, to let my hair dry overnight. I wake up to my pillow soaked and my ankle staining my sheets with dried brown blood. A hummingbird hovers outside my window, ruby-throated.

TEXAS FOREVER

In Austin, someone who looks exactly like the Madonna-pap-smear girl from *Slacker* serves me pistachio ice cream with an extra scoop "just cuz." I try slowing down my speech to a drawl, my power-walk to a stroll. We rent a car and drive out of the city. I can't eat my extra "just cuz" scoop fast enough against the sun. It seeps down the waffle cone, my hand, onto my thigh. I lick my fingers and look out the car window. The billboards tell me that God and Jesus love me lots out here, but I'd never guess from everyone's glares.

WHITE SEATMATES ON CHINA EASTERN FLIGHT 207

"You hear that Thailand's king died? God, I hope the Full Moon Party isn't cancelled."

SIEM REAP

I wake up at 4 a.m. to catch the sunrise at Angkor Wat. I accidentally take more pictures of monkeys and stray cats than temples. I shoot dirty looks at a white couple complaining about all the Asian tourists ruining their selfie in front of a tree. I hear the tree was in *Tomb Raider*. I forget about an old pack of baos in my bag and so all my clothes smell like taro and pork belly. I take pictures of white people taking pictures of local kids for their Instagram. I want to cry when locals ask me where I'm from, because I know they are trying to bring me closer, not push me away. I accidentally sleep through the sunset. I hear it was beautiful.

THE BEACH

You ask if my swimsuit is new and I say, "No." I press a shell to my ear and all I hear is blood.

THE DESERT

What would it be like to die here? What do you want to be when you rot? I want flowers seeping out of my jaw, snaking around my bones. I want something to grow out of me.

THE TOP OF THE MOUNTAIN

It is beautiful because it has nothing to do with you.

WHAT KIND OF ANIMAL ARE YOU? BUZZFEED QUIZ

A jellyfish, because they are soft, free-swimming, blooming, boneless, brainless, breathless, heartless, venomous.

FLORA

It is no surprise that I take care of my plants better than I take care of myself. Plants are more obvious and dramatic in their decay, whereas I can go quietly about my life with minimal food and sleep and care, until it all boils over and under my skin and I realize my stomach and eye sockets and pussy are all cavities.

FAUNA

Recall that high school biology lesson on relationships: mutualistic, commensalistic, parasitic. We were taught these as if they only occur between wild animals in faraway ecosystems: invisible bacteria, sea anemones and clownfish, toothy bugs. Not once did teachers warn us about forming parasitic relationships with our fake friends and gaslighting sweethearts. Not once did we think of ourselves as wild, living organisms. Note how I say "living" instead of "existing." There is a difference.

THINGS THAT HAVE MORE HEARTS THAN ME

Worms, hagfish, octopi, and frogs.

***BLADE RUNNER* (1982)**

Am I human? Even if I am not treated like one?

HER (2013)

What good is my advice, my love, my sex to you without my body?

REAR WINDOW (1954)

Women are mothers or wives. Women like fashion or camping. Women wear dresses or jeans. Women are blonde or brunette. Women die or live to be punished.

VIVRE SA VIE (1962)

Men in film school tell me about this famous film I haven't heard of. "I have," I tell them. "You haven't *really* until you see the 35mm print," men tell me. Men in film school tell me about how their girlfriend "looks *so* much like Anna Karina reincarnated." "But she's still alive," I tell them. "I meant when she was beautiful," men tell me. Men in film school tell me about how their girlfriend who looks *so* much like Anna Karina reincarnated is the star of their short film, "so it's like art imitating life imitating art." "Godard abused his muse," I tell them. "No, he loved her," men tell me.

IN THE MOOD FOR LOVE (2000)

Secrets that I would whisper into the hollow of a tree, covered with mud, on top of a mountain:

- I get more love from my parents than I deserve.
- I am scared that I won't love my child.
- I love my friends more than they love me.
- I was disgusted by my high school boyfriend's "love."
- I think she only liked me because she knew that I would love her.

LOVE

We make pasta and make out to the DVD menu of *The Sopranos* season 2, disc 2 on repeat.

REAL LOVE

After we fight you make up by cooking me sunny-side-up quail eggs on tiny slices of rock-hard baguette. The yolk dribbles out of my mouth and down my chin. I feel a shard of shell nick the lining of my throat. Still, I swallow.

TRUE LOVE

Do not say you would die for me. I would not want to live for you.

CRITERIA FOR CRAZY

Saying no, saying yes, saying nothing, speaking up, asking questions, giving answers, political, medicated, off meds, rehab, rehabilitated, traumatized, drunk, dry, armpit hair, arm hair, leg hair, pubic hair, nipple hair, unibrow hair, upper-lip hair, hairless, crying during movies, laughing during movies, crying, laughing, texting, not texting, emojis, pics, no pics, lots of friends, three friends, fucking, not fucking, makeup, no makeup, push-up bra, sports bra, no bra, kinky, vanilla, no chill, too chill, knowing how to sing the backwards line in Missy Elliott's "Work It."

ACKNOWLEDGEMENTS

Thank you to the editors of *Poor Claudia* (Stacey Tran), *The Fuck of the Century* (Gabrielle Marceau), *Web Safe 2k16* (Ben Sisto and Josephine Livingstone), *Cosmonauts Avenue* (Ann Ward), *The Puritan* (Catriona Wright and A. Zachary), and *The Hart House Review* (Adam Gregory) for featuring some of these pieces online.

Endless love and thanks to:

Ashley Opheim, Jay Ritchie, and Guillaume Morissette.

Christine Shan Shan Hou, A. Zachary, Victoria Long, and Alex Manley.

Mitski, Stacey Tran, Matthew Salesses, and Mark Cugini.

Sarah Chant, Camille Simardone, Marcus Sullivan, Jasmin Yee, Auntie May, Uncle Kris, Prentice Fraser, Anastasia Korolj, Joy Xiang, Jessica J. Lee, and Phoebe Wang.

Mom, Dad, my sisters, my extended family, and my friends.

Adrian and Berkeley.

Sennah Yee is from Toronto, where she writes poetry, prose, and film criticism. She is the author of two chapbooks, *THE AQUARIUM* and *THE GL.A.DE* (Dancing Girl Press), and the children's book *MY DAY WITH GONG GONG* (Annick Press). Her Cinema & Media Studies MA thesis focused on gendered robot design in popular media.

www.sennahyee.com